Read and Play
Diggers

by Jim Pipe

Aladdin/Watts
London • Sydney

digger

Here are two **diggers**.

2

What jobs can a **digger** do?

3

dig

4

A digger can **dig**.

It **digs** a hole.

5

push

A digger
can **push**.

6

It **pushes**
the soil.

smash

8

A digger can **smash** walls.

It is very noisy!

grab

10

This digger can **grab**.

It **grabs** with its claw!

pick up

This digger **picks up** rocks.

It is very strong.

13

load

14

This digger **loads** a truck.

It works fast.

15

scoop

16 This digger **scoops** up rocks.

It has a big shovel.

17

drill

18 This digger **drills** a hole.

cut

This digger **cuts** down trees.

What can it do?

drill

load

push

grab

20 Match the words and pictures.

How many?

Can you count the diggers?

Can you dig?

dig

load

pick up

grab

 22 What can you do like a digger?